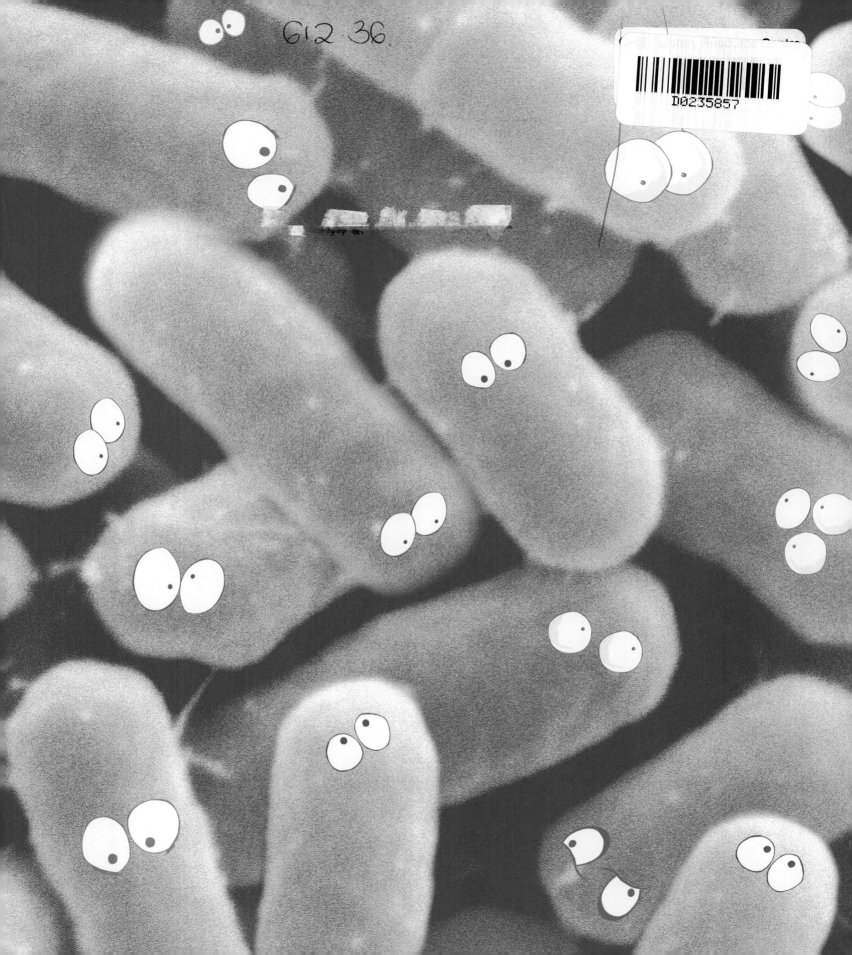

Don't Flush!

Written by
Mary &
Richard Platt

Illustrated by
John Kelly

KINGFISHER

📖 KINGFISHER

First published 2012 by Kingfisher
an imprint of Macmillan Children's Books
a division of Macmillan Publishers Limited
20 New Wharf Road, London N1 9RR
Basingstoke and Oxford
Associated companies throughout the world
www.pacmacmillan.com

Dedicated to Austen

Consultant: Selina Hurley, Assistant Curator
of Medicine, Science Museum, London

ISBN 978-0-7534-3399-7

Copyright © Macmillan Children's Books 2012

1 3 5 7 9 8 6 4 2
1TR/0712/UTD/WKT/140MA

A CIP catalogue record for this book
is available from the British Library.

Printed in China

This product is produced in association with National
Museum of Science and Industry Enterprises Limited.
Royalties from the sale of this product help fund the
Science Museum's exhibitions and programmes.
Science Museum® is a registered trade mark no. 2345143.

Internationally recognized as one of the world's leading
science centres, the Science Museum, London, contains more
than 10,000 amazing exhibits, two fantastic simulator rides and
the astounding IMAX cinema. Enter a world of discovery and
achievement, where you can see, touch and experience real objects
and icons which have shaped the world we live in today.
Visit www.sciencemuseum.org.uk to find out more.

MEET THE POO CREW!

CONTENTS

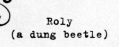

Roly
(a dung beetle)

Pecker
(a pigeon)

Buzz
(a bluebottle)

'Sniffer' Jenkins
(a dog)

Sidney Sewers
(a rat)

LUCKY CHARMS

THE WEE AND

PART EXCHANGE WELCOME!

PLOP SHOP

WAIT! Don't flush... not yet! It's time we took a new look at poo and wee. What we flush away today was precious in the past. People used human and animal waste for washing and beauty treatments, and to make things, such as gunpowder, leather and medicines. Even now, it can help feed us, shelter us and heat our homes. Turn the page to see what amazingly useful things you can do with wee and poo.

Kidneys

Stomach

Small intestine

Large intestine

Bladder

BELL

MANURE FOR HEALTHIER PLANTS

LEATHER

POO PRODUCTION

Poo is what is left of what you eat. Your stomach churns food and adds natural chemicals, so you can absorb its goodness in your small intestine. Your large intestine turns poo from a soup to a firmer paste. Wee makes a shorter journey. Your kidneys produce wee and your bladder stores it.

POO EMPORIUM

EMPORIUM LIT AND POWERED BY POO

THE POO CREW

LUCKY CHARMS

BEAUTY PRODUCTS

MEDICINES

BRICKS

EXPLOSIVES

WATER

ENVELOPES

YOUR GUIDES
In this wee and poo tour, you'll need a guide. Well, five actually. Meet the Poo Crew! Sidney Sewers (rat), Buzz (bluebottle), Pecker (pigeon), Roly (dung beetle) and 'Sniffer' Jenkins (dog) will show you around.

TINNED ARTIST'S POO - REDUCED

WHAT'S IN WASTE?
Wee is mostly water. Just one-twentieth of it is made of salt, plus 70 chemicals that our bodies produce as waste. Poo is three-quarters water, too. Most of the rest is dead bacteria from the gut, or undigested food. There are also small amounts of fats, minerals and proteins.

Water

Bacteria

Fats Proteins

Undigested food

Minerals

GATHERING GOLD

There's money in the sewer! What we flush down the toilet makes valuable fertilizer. As manure, poo helps food plants grow in farm fields. Before chemical fertilizers became available in the 19th century, poo was called 'night soil' and was collected after dark. 'Night soil men' gathered it from city sewers and pits before selling it to farms and markets. This trade continues in a few places, and may expand as the rising cost of fertilizers forces farmers to use manure again.

STINKY MARKETS

Night soil men sold their poo products at markets. When Spanish explorers visited Tenochtitlan (now Mexico City) in 1519, they saw a night soil market. Chinese and Japanese cities also had markets, often near harbours, where night soil boats could be unloaded.

NIGHT SOIL COLLECTION

London night soil men worked in teams of four, always after midnight. The holeman climbed into the sewer and filled a bucket with sludge. The ropeman hauled it up, and two tubmen emptied it into a cart. Their jobs were considered so nasty that they earned double the wage of a skilled worker.

WHAT'S IT WORTH?

City sewage was not the best manure. A 10th-century writer claimed pigeon dung was better for farming. After people's poo, the most valuable poo came from asses, goats, sheep, cattle, pigs and then horses. Even humans were unequal: in 18th-century Japan, the poo of a rich samurai warrior was twice as valuable as that of a poor family.

HUMANURE

Spreading poo and wee on farms and gardens is kinder to the environment than washing sewage away. In regions without sewers, engineers have begun to install composting lavatories, which produce 'humanure'. Composting gets rid of bad smells and harmful germs.

LORDING IT UP

In medieval England, a wealthy lord had the right to fold (fence in) all the sheep and cattle on his land, so that their droppings enriched only his fields. Poorer people, who needed the manure more, hated this rule, which was called a 'folding right'.

FERTILIZER ISLAND

Using night soil as fertilizer ended in the mid-19th century with the discovery of guano – the fertile, dry droppings of seagulls and bats. The Pacific island of Nauru was once a guano mountain. Its mining made the islanders rich, but ruined their home.

HUMAN

ASS

GOAT

SHEEP

PIG

HORSE

GÂRDEN GROWERS

Hauled from city streets and smelly stables, night soil and manure have helped crops to grow tall and strong for years. Pee and poo contain chemicals that plants need for growth and they make the soil lighter, too. Farmers have been boosting their crops with manure for more than 10,000 years — but by the 19th century, gardeners had found many more ingenious uses for what they just called 'muck'.

READY SPREADY GO

Found in fresh manure, the chemical ammonia is strong enough to turn leaves brown, so farmers and gardeners compost (rot) manure for at least six months before spreading it on soil. Dung heats up quickly when it rots, so heaps are kept small to stop them bursting into flames.

PINEÂPPLE PITS

Gardeners used the heat of rotting dung to pamper delicate plants. Pineapples usually flourish only in tropical areas, but by surrounding pots with 'hot beds' of rotting dung, gardeners in chilly northern Europe could grow the fruit.

HOT HÂTCHERS

Hatching eggs normally requires a mother hen's warm belly or an expensive heated incubator (hatching box). Instead, thrifty farmers used to put eggs in straw-filled barrels and warm them with rotting dung. That was hatching on the cheep!

MUSHROOM MIRACLE

Woods and fields have always been a source of delicious mushrooms. However, in the 17th century French farmers found that growing them on dung heaps in dark caves, or sheds, was quicker than gathering them from the wild. This method is also used today to farm some supermarket mushrooms.

WHAT MITE HAVE BEEN

Archaeologists have shown the importance of manure in farming by counting the remains of crops, and tiny insects called dung mites. The Incas, Peru's ancient people, fertilized their corn fields with llama dung – the home and food of these tiny dung mites. In 2,700-year-old mud, corn and mite numbers matched, proving that more dung makes more corn.

NAME CHANGE

Today, sewage is a dirty word, and many people don't want to spread night soil on their fields or gardens. As a result, waste-water engineers now refer to sewage as 'biosolids'. Composted and harmless, biosolids even fertilize the lawn of the White House – home to the US President.

THE HUNT IS ON

On the trail of wild beasts, a piece of pristine poo provides as much information as a footprint. Skilled trackers call animal poo 'scat'. Its size, shape, smell, colour, squishiness and undigested food content are all valuable clues. Together they can tell a hunter which animal dropped the deposit, how big the beast was, what it enjoyed for lunch and how recently the poo was passed.

A MEDIEVAL HUNT

Hunting was the sport of kings in Europe during the Middle Ages (about 1000-1500CE). While the royal party had a picnic, humble trackers went in search of game to hunt. They prized any 'fewmets' (scat) they found, because they could take it to their noble masters.

THE HARBOURER'S JOB

The scat specialist on the hunt was the harbourer. He put any fewmets he found in his shirt or his hunting horn, and then returned to the hunting party. There he presented the poo to his lady, usually at the beginning of a meal. By carefully studying the scat, the noblemen decided which beast to hunt.

WORD OF WARNING!

Be aware that scat can spread disease and parasites. If you track animals and handle their scat, always wash your hands with soap and water straight afterwards.

MODERN TRACKING

Today, few people feed themselves by hunting and killing animals, but tracking skills are still valuable. In game reserves, rangers rely on scat to lead visitors to wildlife they want to see and photograph. Soldiers also learn tracking as a survival skill in remote regions.

ENDANGERED SPECIES

If animals are too rare or too shy to spot in the wild, scientists use scat to trace and count them. In the North Atlantic, fewer than 400 right whales survive. Detection dogs on boats sniff out whale scat, so biologists can check the whales' health.

Goose

Coyote

Rabbit

Rat

WHAT'S THAT SCAT?

Puzzled about who left that pile of poo in your garden? Wildlife books can help you identify four-legged visitors, but a session with a local wildlife trust will be more 'hands-on'. These lifelike, plastic samples can't help you to recognize tell-tale odours, but at least you can carry them in your pocket for side-by-side comparisons.

SCENT OR STINK?

For animals, wee and poo smells are like a television game show – with life-or-death prizes! Creatures use their powerful noses to detect danger or desire. They flee from the droppings of bigger, hungrier species, and pick up on the signals that show an attractive mate is nearby. We humans have learned to use animal scents and stinks to lure the desirable and repel the dangerous.

ÂNIMÂL ÂTTRÂCTION

For a hungry fly, the smell of fresh poo signals 'Dinner is served!' Many mammals have scent glands in their bladders and guts. When they are looking for a mate, these produce chemicals called pheromones, which the opposite sex find hard to resist.

SCÂREDY CÂTS

Determined cats can dig up a garden faster than its owner can repair it. Gardeners fight back with the help of the cat's fierce jungle cousins. *Silent Roar* cat repellent contains extract of lion poo. Its smell has pussycats running for safety.

DUNG DISGUISE

Even clean humans smell strong to animals, so getting dirty makes a good disguise. Some 19th-century African elephant hunters smeared themselves with elephant dung. The smelly camouflage meant they could move unnoticed through a herd and spear them.

LIGHTING Â SMUDGE

Poo was used to keep away midges and mosquitoes long before scientists invented chemical insect repellents. Missouri Indians, Chinese and Egyptian people all lit dung fires when these tiny pests plagued them. European explorers copied them, calling a dung fire a 'smudge'.

DÂNGER ZONE

If you have ever walked a male dog, you will have seen animal smells in action. Each time he lifts his leg to go for a wee, your pet is leaving a message that he is the boss around there. Other species find such smells a threat, and may avoid territory marked with pee or poo.

REINDEER ROUND-UP

Northern peoples of Canada, Alaska and Siberia once tamed wild reindeer using wee. As the deer craved the salty taste of wee, herders laid long lines of it to round them up. This liking for wee makes tame deer a hazard for people weeing in the snow: the deer come running to drink it, and they are big!

13

DOWNSTREAM DIAGNOSIS

Eat a dodgy prawn, and you'll get a fast lesson in diagnosis (identifying illness). Food poisoning changes the urgency of your bathroom visits, and it's one of many complaints that affect your wee and poo. Medieval doctors combined uroscopy (studying wee) with astrology for a diagnosis that was no better than guesswork. Urine tests are still common, but they are now more scientific and accurate.

A WEE CHART

In the past, doctors judged a patient's health by comparing wee samples to a colour chart like this one. Here's an example diagnosis: 'Urine that is thick, reddish and milky shows that there is gout in the upper parts of the body.' Whatever the colour, the treatment was often the same: cutting open a vein to drain blood.

URINE TEST

What does my wee say about me? A change in its appearance and flavour can hint at sickness. Blood in wee suggests the presence of a kidney stone (crystals of wee inside the bladder). Foam may be a sign of kidney damage, and diabetes gives wee a sweet flavour. Laboratory tests reveal much more, including pregnancy, bladder infections, jaundice and thyroid problems.

YOU MUST BE CROÂKING!

In the 1960s, doctors injected live frogs with women's wee to see if they were expecting a baby. Pregnant women's wee contains hormones that can make frogs lay eggs. Today, frogs are not needed: women wee on strips that change colour if they are pregnant.

BOTTLING IT UP

Doctors poured wee into special bottles to sniff, taste and look at it. These uroscopy flasks had thin walls so that the glass did not disguise the colour of the contents. The flasks became a symbol of the medical profession.

Eating beetroot turns your wee pink: try it!

1. Small, hard and lumpy
2. Lumpy, but shaped like a sausage
3. Sausage-shaped, but with a cracked surface
4. Smooth and shaped like a snake or sausage
5. Soft pieces, but with clear edges
6. Fluffy, mushy bits with ragged edges
7. Watery and completely liquid

BRISTOL STOOL SCÂLE

How do you measure poo? For doctors treating gut diseases, it is a serious question. They use the Bristol Stool Scale: a guide to hardness, ranging from constipation (Type 1) through to normal (3 or 4) and diarrhoea (7).

15

DOCTOR DUNG

For *sunus*, the doctors of ancient Egypt, dung and droppings were drugs. Their pills used poo from lions, gazelles, houseflies, ostriches, crocodiles and other animals. Though *sunus*' ideas were mostly mistaken, folk remedies ever since have included poo and wee. Poo may even have a future in modern medicine. Physicians transplant it to heal gut problems that resist other treatments (see page 17).

CROCODILE

HOUSEFLY

GAZELLE

OSTRICH

LION

EGYPTIÂN PHÂRMÂCY

About 3,500 years ago, Egyptian medicine was the best in the world, but *sunus* knew little about what made us ill. They guessed that devils and spirits caused disease. To drive them out of a patient's body they put poo into their prescriptions.

WEE WOUND WÂSH

Aztec warriors in ancient Mexico weed on sword cuts to clean them. Urine from a healthy person is sterile (does not contain germs). It is a safer wound wash than water from a muddy pool. Even today, some soldiers are taught to wee on wounds in an emergency.

16

FOLK MEDICINE

Medical science began to replace magic and superstition 300 years ago, but some people carried on using toilet pharmacy. In 18th century Pennsylvania, USA, German immigrants drank a tea made from 'sheep cherries' (sheep droppings) when they caught measles.

WEE IN THE AYURVEDA

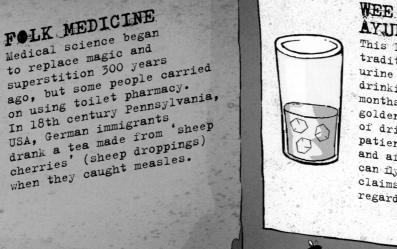

This Indian medical tradition recommends urine as a cure. After drinking it for eight months, patients have a golden glow. Eight years of drinking urine makes patients live for ever, and after ten they can fly like birds! These claims are now widely regarded as false.

FECÂL TRÂNSPLÂNTS

If the helpful bacteria in our guts die, a super-germ called *Clostridium difficile* can take over, with deadly results. In an experimental new treatment, called fecal transplant, doctors inject a solution into patients' bottoms. The solution is made from healthy poo.

MÂKING Â SPLÂSH

No soap? Try washing with wee! Stale wee contains ammonia, a type of detergent that washes out grease. Before soap was invented, the first stage in washing clothes was often a soak in a bucket of wee. In ancient Rome, 2,000 years ago, wee was so valuable that it was collected from public toilets. There was even a tax on urine: some of the money from the sale of wee, for washing, dyeing and other chemical processes, went to the Roman government.

SHORTENED JÂRS

On street corners in Roman cities stood pottery jars for men to wee into. They were called *dolia curta* (shortened jars) because they were cut down to make them convenient for even the shortest Roman to use. Stinky slaves regularly collected the contents.

18

DYEING WITH INDIGO

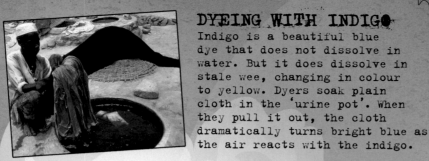

Indigo is a beautiful blue dye that does not dissolve in water. But it does dissolve in stale wee, changing in colour to yellow. Dyers soak plain cloth in the 'urine pot'. When they pull it out, the cloth dramatically turns bright blue as the air reacts with the indigo.

THE FULLER STORY

The contents of each *dolia curta* ended up here, at the fuller's workshop. Fullers processed cloth, but they also took in laundry, such as the togas that Roman citizens wore. Fullers threw the laundry into a big trough, and filled it with wee and water.

SAILORS' SHIRTS

Soap doesn't work in salt water, so seamen on sailing ships saved up 'chamber lye' (a polite name for wee) and soaked their shirts in it. To rinse clothes they used precious drinking water or rainwater. Clothes rinsed in seawater never dry properly.

A SMELLY TAX

When first-century Roman emperor Vespasian decided to put a tax, the *vectigal urinae*, on the wee-wee that the fullers collected, his son Titus complained that it was disgusting. His father threw him a gold coin and asked, 'Does the money smell bad?'

DIRTY WORK

The wealthy fuller didn't actually do the laundry. Instead, he got his slaves to do the dirty work. They climbed in the trough and trod the clothes underfoot. Lots of rinsing in fresh water followed – nobody wants to wear a toga that smells of wee!

DÂNGEROUS DUNG

What's brown, smells and can blow your hand off? It sounds like a bad joke, but in 16th century Europe, exploding dung was a deadly serious issue. Guns were replacing bows and arrows on the battlefield. The gunpowder needed to fire them was scarce and costly. The answer?

Dig up the nearest dunghill!

Farmyards, sties, chicken coops and animal pens were a rich source of saltpetre.

PRECIOUS POWDER

Making an explosion required fuel, and an 'oxidizer' – a chemical that supplies masses of oxygen. In gunpowder, the oxidizer was saltpetre, or 'nitre' (potassium nitrate). It was found in a crude form in wee and poo. Saltpetre-men made a pile of dung, and poured wee onto it for months, until white crystals appeared on the surface. They checked, by licking them, that the crystals were of saltpetre, which had a 'cold' taste. Mixing the crystals with water and wood ash purified them. Then boiling down the liquid concentrated and dried the saltpetre.

This is how they made saltpetre in 1580. The long mounds are dung heaps. An awful lot of dung is needed to make just a little saltpetre.

MÂKING GUNPOWDER

Saltpetre alone didn't go 'BANG!' To make it explosive, it had to be mixed with charcoal, and with a yellow chemical called sulphur. The quantities of each were vital for a satisfying and noisy blast. Making the powder was dangerous work. Millers ground the three ingredients separately to a fine powder before carefully mixing them into gunpowder. Then they took great care to avoid igniting it. Iron tools often create sparks, so workers handled the powders using copper or wood tools and containers. Leather covered the factory floors, and workers wore special slippers. Despite these precautions, deadly explosions were common.

The correct proportions for making gunpowder:

Charcoal:
3 parts

Sulphur:
2 parts

Saltpetre:
15 parts

SÂLTPETRE-MEN

Officials called 'the king's saltpetre-men' collected the dung needed to make gunpowder. Special laws gave them the power to remove dung heaps, the floors of stables and other pooey places. Everyone hated them because they took the manure that farmers needed to make their crops grow, and they never repaired the floors they tore up.

The ladies of Selma may have weed into a pot like this (left), decorated with a picture of a hated northern general.

PEE INTO POWDER

When America's southern states fought the north in the country's civil war, they soon ran short of gunpowder. As a result, an official in an Alabama town posted this advert in a local newspaper in 1862: 'The ladies of Selma are respectfully requested to preserve all their chamber lye (urine)... for the purpose of making nitre. Wagons with barrels will be sent around for it.' The message caused much amusement.

DING DONG DUNG

What's brown and sounds like a bell? It may be no more than a bad riddle, but the answer – 'dung' – plays an important part in casting (shaping) bells. Nor is this the only use for wee and poo in the foundry. About 900 years ago, Viking swordsmiths made their finest blades using goose poo. Even today, wee-soaked soil adds a unique black finish to Bidriware – metal ornaments made from the stinky soil of a famous fortress.

MIXING LOAM
Moulds used in shaping bells are made from loam – a mixture of dung, clay, sand and goat hair. The bell-founders shape loam into the mould's two parts, forming the inside and outside.

PERFECT CASTING
To get the casting underway, bell-makers melt metal at 900°C. They pour this liquid metal into the mould – a container the exact shape of the bell. Pouring the metal is the most skilled part of bell-casting.

HEAVY METAL
As the metal flows into the mould, its intense heat burns away the dung that was mixed into the loam. This leaves tiny channels in the mould. The hot metal makes the air inside the mould swell suddenly. The channels created by the dung allow the expanding air to escape without cracking the mould.

Goat hair

Horse manure

Sand

22

SWORD SAGA

In a Viking saga (story), a blacksmith made his finest sword, named Mímungr, by feeding scraps of lesser swords to his geese. Then he added goose droppings to the metal he melted to cast Mímungr. Scientists guess that traces of other chemicals in the goose dung really strengthened the sword.

QUENCHING DAMASCUS

Medieval blacksmiths hardened red-hot metal by quenching (cooling) it in water or wee. The best swords came from Damascus, where blacksmiths insisted on wee from red-headed boys. But they may have spread this story to hide the true secret of their superior blades.

BIDRIWARE

The Indian makers of this fancy metalware coat it with soil dug from the darkest corners of the walls of Bidar fort. Visitors have weed in these spots for centuries, and chemicals in the rich, smelly soil instantly blacken the metal's surface.

Pouring molten metal into loam mould

LIBERTY BELL

When bell-casting isn't perfect, the faults are not always obvious. The USA's Liberty Bell was cast in London at the Whitechapel Bell Foundry. When it was rung in Philadelphia for the first time, a crack appeared in its side. Today – still cracked – it is more famous than any faultless American bell!

MIXING IT

Mud bricks are mostly made of... well, mud. But mud on its own cracks when it dries. Adobe builders mix in animal dung or straw to add strength and stop cracks. Dung contains fine fibres from undigested plants, and also helps to make the mud soft and easily moulded.

DUNG IT YOURSELF

In some of the world's hot, dry places, builders rely on dung. It holds up roofs and keeps out the heat. Dung is a vital ingredient in muddy bricks called adobe. They were the first bricks ever made. They supported the ancient world's greatest structures, such as the famous walls of the city of Babylon, built more than 2,500 years ago. Adobe bricks are still used to create homes that are cool in the sun, but warm during nippy nights.

BRICKING IT

To stick adobe bricks together, builders use more of the same type of mud. The walls they create are sturdy, but not very waterproof. Overhanging roofs of straw or iron sheeting stop rain from turning bricks back to mud.

MOULDING THE MUD

Mud bricks are moulded – shaped in a wooden frame. It is messy, slow, hard work. Newly moulded bricks are left to dry for about three days. Then they are stacked for a month to harden before use.

24

SHIBÂM

The world's first high-rise buildings were made from adobe bricks. About 500 of them still stand in the town of Shibam in Yemen, Arabia. The tallest is 30m high. Shibam's unusual homes were built upwards to protect their owners from warlike neighbours.

WÂTTLE ÂND DÂUB

Even in damp, northern Europe, dung makes a useful building material. Mixed with mud, it creates daub. This thick, brown coating is smeared on wattle – woven wooden panels that form the walls of traditional, wood-framed buildings.

POO PLÂSTER

Adobe buildings are coated with a mud-and-dung plaster to fill cracks and keep out the rain. Some adobe builders believe that adding horse wee to the plaster helps to protect it from damage. 'Neigh' way!

BRICKS IN EGYPT

Tomb paintings from ancient Egypt show builders mixing and moulding bricks. People with better jobs looked down on them. One wrote that the builders 'work outside naked, kneading excrement (poo) to make bricks, then eating bread... without washing their hands.'

TÂN YOUR HIDE

In the 19th century, people didn't need good eyesight to find a tannery – they just followed their nose. Turning animal skins into leather required a special, stinky ingredient – dog poo. It contains bacteria (tiny bugs) that made the leather soft and smooth. Tanners called this poo 'pure', and collecting it from city streets was the job of the 'pure finder'.

PURE FINDERS

Collecting dog poo was quite a good job! During the 1850s, in London, men who worked as pure finders were better off than those who collected and sold rags and bones. Tanneries paid a shilling (5p) for each bucket of pure, and this was enough to buy three large bread loaves.

TAKE THE BÂTE

To soften the very best leather, tanners soaked hides in 'bate': a sloshy poo-mud. They made bate by tipping poo into a tub, adding water and kneading it with their feet. Then they tossed in the hides (animal skins) and trod them underfoot for several hours.

26

DOG'S DINNER

Street collections were not the only source of pure. Tanners also bought it from kennels, and many kept dogs themselves. The dogs worked hard for their keep. Besides supplying pure, they also tore the last strips of flesh from the animal hides before tanning could begin.

BALD BEGINNINGS

Scraping the skins with a blunt, curved knife removed any unwanted hair before the bating process.

INUIT TÂNNING

In America's frozen north, Inuit people tanned animal skins using wee, which they collected in ice troughs during the winter. Other native American groups used wee in tanning, sometimes mixing it with crushed animal brains. Fat in the brains made the leather soft and supple.

WHITE OUT

Tanners paid more for white poo because it did not stain the leather. Dishonest pure finders cheated them by rolling regular, brown poo in ground-up chalk.

THE END RESULT

After bating, tanners washed the leather many times, but sometimes not enough to remove the smell of the pure. Leather dealers checked for this by sniffing or licking the hides they bought. This 'trick of the trade' was no longer needed after chemical tanning replaced the bating process in the late 19th century.

MESSY MÂKEOVER

Are you worth it? Do you deserve to be smothered in wee and poo? Of course you do! In search of beauty, anything goes. Skin and hair products have an ancient connection to the dung heap. Beauticians and barbers used wee and poo to lighten and whiten, to make hair grow, and also to make it fall out. Even today, some cosmetics include urea and ammonia, which are found in wee.

CROC SKIN
In his medical text book of the first century CE, Greek pharmacist Dioscorides recommended face cream containing crocodile dung 'for colouring the face and making it shine'. He warned of fakes, made from the poo of rice-fed starlings.

Today, a Japanese company sells a nightingale-poo face cream.

BOTTLE BLONDE
For the women of 16th-century Venice, blonde was beautiful. They combed *bionda* (a mix of lemon juice and stale wee) into their hair. Then they lay in the sun, shading their pale skin with the cut-off rim of a hat. Together, sunshine and *bionda* acted as a bleach to turn the hair lighter.

HÂNDS DOWN
German doctor Johann Wecker wrote a popular beauty manual in the 17th century. One of his top tips was smearing fingernails with a mix of 'arsenic and dog turd' in order to lighten them.

JENKINS

BIONDA

WHÂLE WÂSTE

Tiny amounts of ambergris give a unique scent to the finest perfumes. Grey and waxy, ambergris floats into the ocean in the poo of sperm whales. Washed ashore, it's as valuable as gold.

MOUSETÂCHES

During the 18th century, German men who longed for droopy moustaches were advised to smear mouse droppings under their noses. The same remedy was supposed to cure dandruff, too.

NIGHTLY REFILLS

Doves, asses, camels, cows, swallows, mice, cats, rats, rabbits and goats have all provided the raw material for hair and skin care. But human wee was always popular in times past - perhaps because there was always a pot of it under the bed.

TRÂDITIONÂL TÂTTOOS

Inuit people created their own tattoos using a mixture of wee and soot. They pulled a thread through the mix, then used a needle to pass it under the skin. It may be possible that urea, a natural chemical found in wee, helped to stop the skin getting infected.

The soft drink *Gauloka Peya* ('drink from the land of cow') is made from distilled cow urine mixed with water and herbs. Flavours include orange, rose and lemon. The Hindu group that sells it says, 'It is like any regular sweet drink, without the harmful side effects', but many doctors disagree with this.

BÂCKSIDE BUFFET

Poo on a plate? No thank you! It may sound sickening, but many rare and highly prized foods from around the world get their unusual flavours through being processed with dung. Drinking wee is more common. In fact, you probably drank some today, in your tap water. A few people go further, glugging down their own wee by the glass as a wacky health cure. Ice with that? Yes please!

ICELAND
As winter draws in, Icelanders with smoke houses light a sheep dung fire, and hang a leg of lamb above it. The smoked delicacy is called *Hangikjöt* ('hanging meat'). It's a popular Christmas treat.

INDONESIA
The world's most expensive coffee, *Kopi Luwak*, is made thanks to wild tree cats called palm civets. When these cats eat coffee berries, chemicals in their guts remove the bitterness of the beans inside. Workers collect the beans from civet droppings, then wash, dry and roast them.

DRINKING URINE

In small amounts, fresh human urine is harmless and safe to drink. It is even a traditional medicine in India (see page 17). Those in the West who drink their own wee, for its supposed health benefits, say it tastes better when chilled. Cheers!

WÂTER RECYCLING

Worldwide, most city water contains what was once wee. In Windhoek, Namibia, tap water is made from recycled sewage. The water authorities purify river water, which includes the sewage from towns upstream.

FRANCE

A traditional French hot drink, *Chocolat Ambré*, contains ground up ambergris. This precious flavour, which is also used in perfume, is harvested from sperm whale poo.

AMERICA

During the 18th century, California Indians who ate the cactus fruit *pitahaya* could not digest the tiny seeds. Collected from their poo, the seeds were delicious when roasted and ground up.

MOROCCO

Moroccan goats climb argan trees to eat the fruit, but they cannot digest the stones inside. Herders pick the stones from goat dung. They crush the pits to make tasty argan oil, which is sold for cooking and cosmetics.

MUCK, MYTH & MÂGIC

Embrace the magic power of poo! People from the past believed it brought good luck, so they worshipped dung gods and goddesses. It's easy to see why. Their lives depended on crops. Wee and poo enriched the soil, keeping crops growing and hungry mouths fed. Today, just a few cultures celebrate the tradition of poo worship. But many of us still say 'that means good luck' when a bird poos on our shoulder.

STERCUTIUS

This ancient Roman god of poo was connected with manuring the soil. He got his name from *stercus*, the word for dung in the Latin language that Romans spoke. Greeks worshipped him as Saturn, the god of agriculture.

SÂCRED SCÂRÂB

Ancient Egyptians worshipped a black beetle because it rolled dung balls – just as the god Ra rolled the sun across the sky each day. In one of his forms, Ra appears as a scarab (dung) beetle.

CLOÂCINÂ

This Roman coin shows sewer godess Cloacina. Her shrine was next to the *Cloaca Maxima*, the great drain she protected. Rome's sewage flowed down it into the River Tiber.

LUCKY LANDING

Many superstitious people think that bird poo landing on clothes brings luck. This belief may have begun with *stercomancy* – the art of telling people's fortunes by studying the seeds found in dung.

32

KUMÂLÂK

On the patterned *kumalak* playing cloth, shamans (holy men) of Kazakhstan used to tell villagers' fortunes using 41 dried sheep droppings. Sadly, modern *kumalak* sets use 41 counters or beads instead.

HOLY COW!

Hindus consider the cow to be a sacred animal, and the cow god *Kamadhenu* can grant any wish. At the January harvest festival in India, girls honour him with *Gobbemmalu* - brilliantly decorated cow droppings.

KIN NO UNKO

Japanese people buy gold-coated *kin no unko* (golden poo) charms to share in the luck the toilet gods promise (see right). But they are also enjoying a pun (a word joke). In Japanese, the words 'poo' and 'luck' start with the same 'oon' sound.

TOILET GOD

Benjo-Kami is a Japanese spirit from the Shinto religion, who lives in and protects the family toilet. Singer Kana Uemura made the god more famous in 2011 with a hit song about cleaning her grandma's toilet!

Dinosaur coprolites are prehistoric monsters: a *Tyrannosaurus rex* dropping can be 50cm long! Within these chunky fossils, bits of bone, teeth, wood, leaves, seeds, fish scales and shells survive to teach us about dino dining. Burrows in coprolites can also help identify prehistoric dung beetles.

Dinosaur coprolite

POO OF THE PÂST

For scientists who study the past, there's a clue in the poo. We can learn what dinosaurs ate from what passed through their guts. Dropped more than 100 million years ago, dino dumps hardened into rock-like coprolites (dung stones). Poo can tell us a lot about recent history. By digging up our ancestors' toilets, archaeologists have made us rethink our ideas about how humans spread across the globe.

Microscope

Diamond-tipped saw

DUNG DISCOVERY

Medieval people called coprolites 'bezoar stones', and believed they cured a variety of medical problems. English fossil hunters William Buckland and Mary Anning were the first to guess what they really were, and Buckland named them coprolites in 1829.

PÂLÂEOSCÂTOLOGISTS

To look inside a dinosaur coprolite, palaeoscatologists (the scientists who study them) cut off thin slices using a diamond-tipped saw (left) and smooth them flat and shiny. A microscope (far left) magnifies the specimens, which are so thin that light shines straight through.

CÂVE POO BREÂKTHROUGH

American archaeologist Dennis Jenkins used 14,300-year-old human poo from a cave in Oregon, USA, to show that Asian people reached North America 1,200 years earlier than people previously thought. DNA (see page 46) in the poo revealed the cave-dwellers' origins.

Dennis Jenkins

PEOPLE'S POO

You could break a toe on a dinosaur coprolite, but the human version is more like something you may step in. Archaeologists restore the original texture and smell of people's poo by soaking it in cleaning solutions. What they find inside can reveal the diet of the person, indicating whether they were rich or poor.

35

FLÂMING FUEL

On the treeless plains of the American West, wood was too valuable to make into fires. To cook and stay warm, settlers burned buffalo poo instead. With 60 million buffalo, each dropping three bucketfuls a day, there was no shortage. Cowboys didn't invent dung fires. They copied the ways of native Americans. Even today, dung warms the poor and cooks their food in places where other fuel is scarce.

MEÂDOW MUFFINS

Settlers had many names for buffalo dung. 'Meadow muffins' was the most polite. The French called dung 'cow-wood'. Each autumn, settler families spent at least two weeks picking up meadow muffins to burn during the winter. Snow made collection impossible until the spring thaw.

WOMEN'S WORK

Collecting fuel was traditionally women's work, and popular songs made fun of women who were too proud for the job. In the words of one, '...look at her now with a pout on her lips; as daintily, with her fingertips; she picks for the fire some buffalo chips'.

BURNING BRIGHT

Dung burned with a stinking smoke if it was damp, but dry dung burned well in a good wind. Though a dung fire never got very hot, it had one huge advantage over wood. Dung did not spit sparks that could burn clothes or set fire to a teepee or a settler's wagon.

CÂMEL CRÂZY

As a desert animal, the camel has to conserve water. Its guts squeeze every drop from digested food, so camel poo burns on a fire without needing to be dried first. Wherever camels graze, their owners collect the dung for fires. This girl is carrying a bowlful of dung at India's Pushkar camel fair.

Dung was burned regularly in order to get campfires sizzling in the American West.

POO PROBLEMS

Dung is not a perfect fuel. Its smoky flame creates indoor air pollution and can cause lung problems. Plus, a dung fire is like burning food to cook food. If alternative fuels were available, dung could fertilize fields instead, making crops grow better.

IT'S A GAS

One terrifying night in 1847, a giant explosion shook London's foggy streets. According to reports, a 'vast flame' roared from a sewer, spreading 'an unbearable stench'. The cause was the gas given off by rotting wee and poo. Today, we harvest sewer gas, or 'biogas', which is an environmentally-friendly alternative to fossil fuels such as coal and oil.

ÂNUDDER PROBLEM

Biogas forms in a cow's guts. Using collectors such as this balloon, scientists guess that the world's cows make 100 million tonnes of methane gas each year. If we could harvest it, this could help replace fossil fuels. But we can't, so cow farts continue to warm our climate.

A pipe takes toilet waste to the digester. Garden waste can be shovelled in, too.

FEEDING TIME

Biogas can be made from all kinds of waste, but to make lots of gas requires lots of waste. In home biogas systems, the toilet feeds into the digester (see page 39). However, big commercial systems use waste from farms: wee and poo from cows, pigs and hens.

EXPLODING SEWERS

Sewer explosions regularly rocked city streets in the past. They happened most often when workers who were cleaning or repairing sewers struck matches or lit candles. Sewers rarely explode today because they have vents that release gases, so that they do not build up to dangerous levels.

ÂNAEROBIC DIGESTER

To turn wee and poo into useful biogas, microbes (tiny bacteria) have to digest it. They make more gas if there is no air, so biogas digesters are built to keep the atmosphere out. This is why they are called 'anaerobic' digesters: anaerobic means 'free of air'.

A do-it-yourself digester at work

BURNING BIOGÂS

The gas from a backyard digester burns well in an ordinary cooking stove. However, gas from big commercial plants is purified before it is fed into the pipes leading to homes. It may also be burned at the plant to generate electricity.

BÂCKYÂRD BIOGÂS

You too could power your cooker with poo! All you need to do is fill a concrete-lined tank with sewage. A big plastic membrane is used to keep air out and gas in. A pipe takes the gas to your house. China is a world leader in biogas energy, installing about four million of these family biogas units each year.

39

POOPER PÂPER

Making paper usually means crushing trees in giant machines. But there is an alternative way to get paper from plants: just feed them to hungry animals. The beasts' teeth and guts grind and digest the green plants. What is left of the meal emerges at the other end, ready to turn into soft, smooth paper sheets.

POO PECKERS

Mammals that eat plants have special guts to digest tough leaves, but a lot of what goes in their mouths still comes out unchanged. Birds and insects know this, and flock to fresh poo to pick tasty morsels from the fibres.

Elephants produce a wheelbarrow-load of dung each day

Dung is washed and boiled for several hours

Simple mixers make the fibres shorter

These dung balls contain equal amounts of fibre

POO CÂNOE

The Welsh makers of Sheep Poo Paper have found a novel use for it. Layered with beeswax and waterproof resin, it covers a home-made canoe. The daring canoeists plan to paddle their boat from the UK to France to raise money for charity.

PERFECT PÂPER

In the digestive system of elephants, half the fibre they eat passes straight through their guts. Because it contains so much fibre, elephant poo is the ideal raw material for paper. Processing removes smells, cleans and sterilizes the plant fibres and separates them from unwanted material.

BAMBOO POO

China's Chengdu panda breeding centre once had a giant problem: disposing of two tonnes of panda poo a day. But now they make it into paper to raise money for the centre. Pandas digest just 20 per cent of their bamboo diet, and the paper smells of bamboo.

Wetting each ball spreads out the fibres, and sifting through a fine mesh creates a sogey paper sheet

Drying sheets in the sun creates the finished paper

WRITE-ON!

Poo paper looks and smells like any other good quality, handmade paper. You can write, draw or print on it. Although poo paper is an expensive novelty, making it helps support communities by providing jobs and attracting tourist visits.

BRUSHSTROKES

For the world's very first artists, painting with wee was simply practical: it was always available in the dark caves where they worked. Today's painters use wee and poo for more creative reasons. They know these materials are more shocking than paint. They use them as a reminder of their culture and roots. Or they enjoy the joke of making priceless art from worthless stuff.

CA-CA-CAVE PAINTINGS

Working more than 40,000 years ago, early artists painted elegant images of the beasts they hunted. Instead of paint they used mud in shades of red, yellow, brown and black. To stick it to rocks, or to the walls and ceilings of caves, they needed some liquid, so many of them used wee.

ROMAN REMAINS

Belgian artist Wim Delvoye built *Cloaca* as a 'useless machine' to show up how pointless modern life is. Named after the Roman sewer (see page 32), *Cloaca* is an artificial gut. Food that goes in at one end emerges at the other as lifelike poo.

42

MUCKY MONKS

Illuminated manuscripts (painted books) of the Middle Ages hide a smelly secret. The monks who created them got their materials from the monastery *reredorter* (their communal toilet). Urine contains a chemical that, when heated, fixed the books' colours or made them brighter.

MÂSKING THE POO

The Gurunsi people of west Africa's Burkina Faso make and paint masks that are world famous and highly valuable. The masks represent a range of spirits and animals. Gurunsi artists create white paint from lizard poo, which they collect out of the animals' burrows.

POO INTO MOO!

British sculptor Sally Matthews was brought up on a farm, where there was never a shortage of cow dung. She used eight buckets of it – along with sheep's wool and wire – to build this amazingly lifelike cow. Thanks to the materials, it even *smells* like a cow.

AND BEYOND...

If you have read this far, you will know the value of wee and poo. We need to use them wisely because our planet's resources are shrinking. In space, astronauts already practise what we must all learn – drinking each and every drop of water time after time. On Earth below, inventive wee and poo projects show the way forward.

Space toilets are cunningly designed to hoover up the weightless wee and poo.

The recycled wee that astronauts drink is purer than our tap water.

FREEZE-DRIED WEE
Some space missions just dumped wee and poo, and this sewage still orbits Earth today. Colliding with it can do as much damage to a spacecraft as a truck moving at motorway speed.

RECYCLING URINE
The risk of crashing into their own bodily waste is not the only reason astronauts have been recycling it since 2008: shipping water up to a space station costs £7,000 a glass! The spacecraft's water recovery system filters and purifies not only wee, but washing water and sweat as well.

IOWA MANURE

It takes a lot of energy to make fertilizers, and as oil prices rise, so too do farmers' costs. Farmers in Iowa, USA, are saving money – and the environment – by replacing chemical fertilizers with traditional manure.

THE POWER OF POO

Making methane (see page 38) is not just about backyard biogas burps. At Didcot in Oxfordshire, UK, a shiny new anaerobic digester is supplying gas to about 200 homes. It is powered by waste from the region's sewage system.

NEW LOOS

In this slum in Brazil there is no proper sewer. Worldwide, four out of ten families do not have decent toilets. Inventors are competing to build cheap toilets that don't waste water, and to safely convert poo into fuel and fertilizer.

BOLIVIAN CLEAN-UP

Poo stops poisons reaching Bolivia's water supply. In streams flowing from abandoned mines, poo pits filled with llama dung are too polluted to drink. But passing the water through the mineral-filled llama reaction removes much the mineral waste.

DIRTY WORDS

adobe
A dried mud brick.

ambergris
A grey material produced in the guts of whales, used in food and perfume.

archaeologist
A scientist who learns about the past by digging up the remains and possessions of people from long ago.

arsenic
A poisonous, metal-like chemical.

bacteria (plural of 'bacterium')
Minute creatures that cause decay or disease in plants and animals.

bamboo
A type of giant grass that grows quickly.

biogas
A fuel gas produced by biological waste and sewage.

biosolid
Sewage made harmless and spread as a fertilizer.

bladder
The organ in an animal's body that collects and stores wee.

camouflage
A pattern on the surface of an animal, building or vehicle that makes it less easy to see.

charcoal
A black, smokeless fuel made by heating wood.

climate change
The way our planet's climate is warming, and becoming less easy to predict, caused by the burning of fossil fuels.

concentrate
To make a solution stronger by reducing the amount of liquid.

coprolite
Fossilized animal dung — for example, that of a dinosaur.

dandruff
Flakes of dead skin that fall from the scalp (surface of head).

decay
The breaking down and rotting of dead things.

diabetes
A medical condition that makes people store sugar in their bodies, causing thirst and constant weeing.

dissolve
To mix something solid into a liquid so that no particles of the solid can be seen.

distillation
Separation — by heating — of a mixture of liquids that boil at different temperatures.

DNA
A biological code, stored in living cells, that controls how plants and animals live, grow and reproduce.

donor
A person who gives something, such as a part of their body, to another person.

dye
A coloured substance that can change the colour of materials it mixes with.

fertilizer
A material that makes soil richer, so that plants can grow in it better.

fortune-telling
Predicting what will happen to someone in the future.

fossil fuels
Fuels extracted from the planet, such as gas, coal and oil. These materials formed hundreds of millions of years ago from the remains of ancient forests.

fuller
A worker who treats cloth, after it is woven, to clean and thicken it.

gunpowder
An explosive powder.

guts
The digestive system of an animal, passing through the whole length of its body.

herder
Someone who looks after a group of farm animals.

hormone
A signalling chemical that moves around the body in fluids such as blood.

immigrant
Someone who leaves their homeland behind and goes to another country to start a new life.

jaundice
A condition of the liver that causes yellowing of the skin.

manure
Animal dung spread on soil to make it better for growing plants and crops.

mate
The partner that a person or animal chooses, with the aim of starting a family.

membrane
A thin layer or wall enclosing something, or keeping two different things apart.

microbe
Something other than a poison that causes disease or bad health. A germ, basically.

Middle Ages
Also called medieval, the period of European history between ancient and modern times: approximately 1000-1500CE.

mould
A container shaped to enclose a hardening paste – such as mud – so that, when set, the paste takes the shape of the mould.

night soil
Solid human waste taken from toilets and streets at night.

orbit
To move in a circular path around the Earth, without falling to the ground or flying off into space.

oxidizer
A substance that causes another substance to have a chemical reaction with oxygen.

palaeoscatologists
Scientists who study preserved poo to learn about the lives of people or animals from the past.

pollution
Waste from human activity that harms air, soil or water.

prehistoric
Something that existed or took place before recorded history began.

prescription
A form from a doctor asking a pharmacist to supply a healing drug.

repellent
Something unpleasant that makes an animal go away.

sacred
Having special importance in a religion.

saltpetre
A white, powdery chemical that, when mixed with many other substances and lit, makes them burn more quickly.

scat
The droppings of an animal.

sewage
Liquid and solid waste from the human gut and bladder.

sewer
A pipe for carrying sewage.

shrine
A small place for prayer and worship in a temple, home or street.

sterile
Not containing any germs.

sunu
A doctor in ancient Egypt.

thyroid
An organ in the neck that produces growth hormones.

transplant
To move an organ or other material from one person's body to another.

uroscopy
Looking at urine to try and identify an illness in a person or animal.

vent
An opening through which gases can escape.

INDEX

PICTURE CREDITS

The Publisher would like to thank the following for permission to reproduce their material. Every care has been taken to trace copyright holders. However, if there have been unintentional omissions or failure to trace copyright holders, we apologise and will, if informed, endeavour to make corrections in any future edition.

t = top; b = bottom; c = centre; l = left; r = right

Cover Shutterstock/christi180884 and pages 6 Getty/SSPL; 7t Art Archive(AA)/Real Biblioteca de lo Escorial; 7b Alamy/WEPL; 9t Science Photo Library (SPL)/Power and Syred; 9b Shutterstock/Vacclav; 11t Getty AWL; 11tr Dr Rosalind M. Roland D.V.M., Right Whale Conservation Medicine Program, New England Aquarium; 11ctl, ctr, bcl & bcr Acorn Naturalists, California; 13b Shutterstock/Andreas Gradin; 14 AA/University Library, Prague/Dagli Orti; 15tl FLPA/Pete Oxford/Minden; 15tr Jpbl301/Wikipedia;17 SPL/Dr Tony Brain, 19tl Superstock/Eye Ubiquitous; 19b Getty/de Agostini; 20 Heritage Images/Oxford Science Archive; 21 Alabama Department of Archives and History, Montgomery, Alabama; 23t Pictures From History; 23b Randhirreddy @ wik; 25ct Getty/Lonely Planet; 25lc Alamy/Paul

Felix Photography; 25br AA/Dagli Orti; 26 Alamy/world History Archive; 27 AA/Kharbine-Tapabor Collection, Folas; 31 Alamy/ frans lemmens; 33t Alamy/RIA Novosti; 33cr Alamy/Tim Gainey; 34 SPL/Ted Kinsman; 35 Jim Barlow/University of Oregon; 37t Shutterstock/Jeremy Richards; 37b Getty/James L. Stanfield; 38 Corbis/Marcus Brindicci/Reuters; 40 www.SheepPooPaper.com; 41 Shutterstock/Hung Chung Chih; 42 With the kind permission of Wim Delvoye, Antwerp; 43t Alamy/Worldwide Picture Library; 43b Getty/Barcroft Media; 45tl Alamy/AGStockUSA; 45tr SPL/James King-Holmes/scitechimage; 45c Getty/Universal Pictures; 45bl Alamy/James Brunker.

The authors would also like to thank the following: Paul Barreau for clarifying an internet myth about dung hurling at the Camel Cup races. Melanie Brown of Biophase for her advice on Bioremediation. Ian Chilvers for his help with art. Jean Smoke of HTI for her information on the company's remarkable water-filtering membranes. Professor Paul Younger of Newcastle University, and Associate Professor Bod Nairn of the University of Oklahoma for their information concerning bioremediation and llama dung.

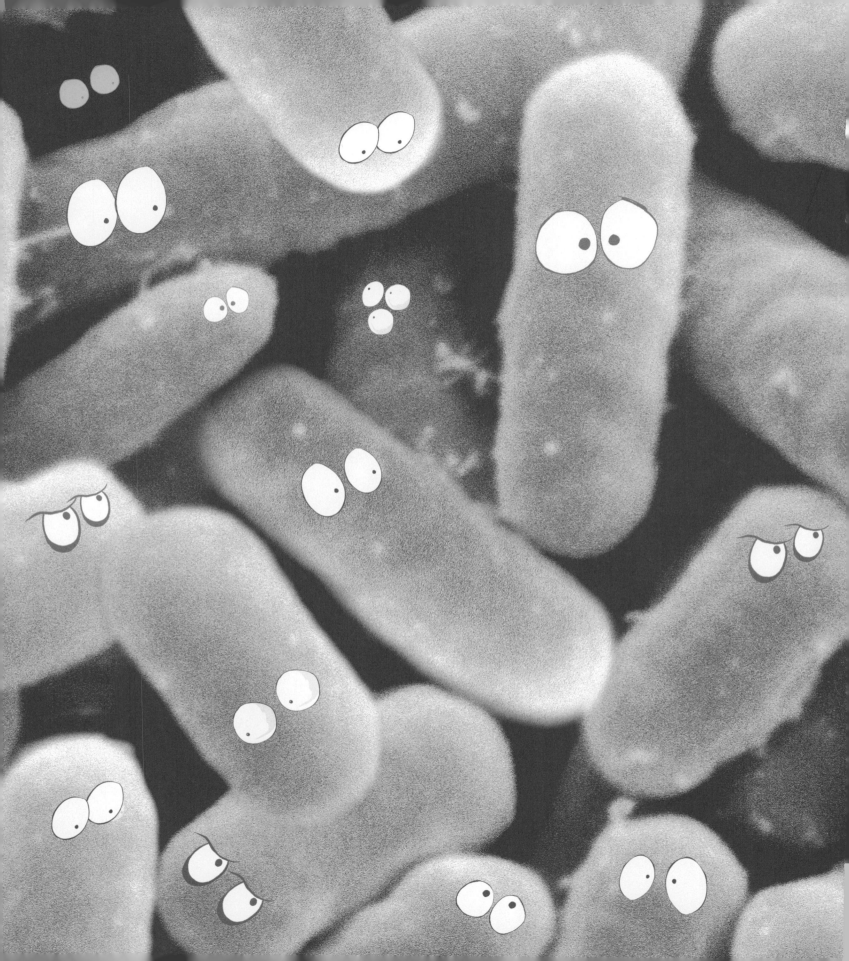